FOLK-SONGS FOR CHOIRS 1

Twelve arrangements for unaccompanied mixed voices

Edited by John Rutter

Music Department
OXFORD UNIVERSITY PRESS
Oxford and New York

Oxford University Press, Walton Street, Oxford OX2 6DP, England
Oxford University Press, 200 Madison Avenue, New York, NY 10016, USA

Oxford New York Toronto
Delhi Bombay Calcutta Madras Karachi
Petaling Jaya Singapore Hong Kong Tokyo
Nairobi Dar es Salaam Cape Town
Melbourne Auckland
and associated companies in
Berlin Ibadan

Oxford is a trade mark of Oxford University Press

Folk-songs for Choirs 1 gathers together into a single volume twelve
unaccompanied mixed-voice arrangements of folk-songs from the British
Isles and North America that have hitherto been available only as separate
leaflets. The songs range widely in regional origin and character, and their
settings reflect this diversity. Three 'classic' arrangements are included:
Greensleeves by Vaughan Williams, *My sweetheart's like Venus* by Holst, and
the *Londonderry Air* by Percy Grainger. The other arrangements are more
recent; two of them are the work of Sir David Willcocks and four are by
John Rutter.

The companion volume *Folk-songs for Choirs 2* contains a further thirteen
unaccompanied mixed-voice arrangements, all of them of folk-songs from
the British Isles.

Contents

for the Schola Cantorum of Oxford

1. AMONG THE LEAVES SO GREEN, O

English folk-song
collected by
Cecil J. Sharp
arranged by
JOHN BYRT

Also available separately (X 137)

2. BUSHES AND BRIARS

English folk-song
collected by
R. Vaughan Williams
arranged by
DONALD JAMES

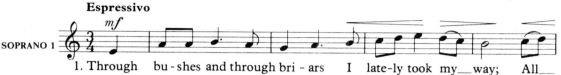

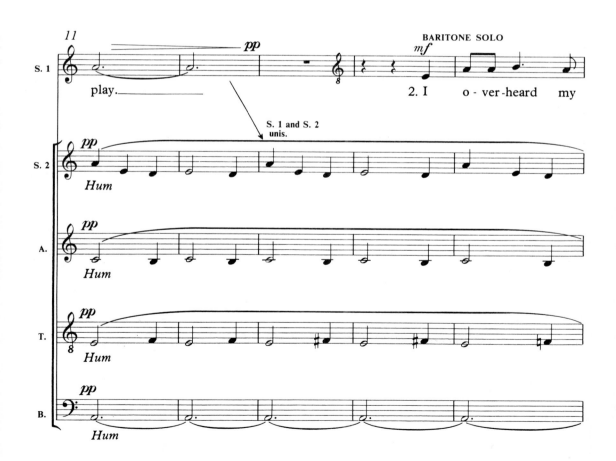

3. BLACK SHEEP

Traditional American lullaby
arranged by
JOHN RUTTER

Melody and words collected by Alan Lomax and taken from *The Folk Songs of North America* (Cassell & Co. Ltd.) by permission of Alan Lomax.
See footnote to *Sourwood Mountain* (p. 75)

for Robin

4. BOBBY SHAFTOE

Scottish folk-song
arranged by
DAVID WILLCOCKS

No. 5 of *Five Folk-Songs* arranged by David Willcocks (OUP)

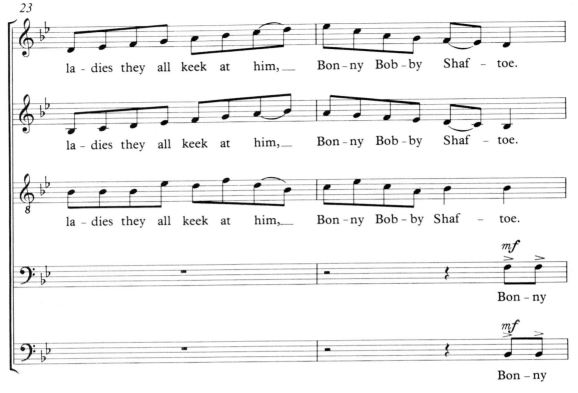

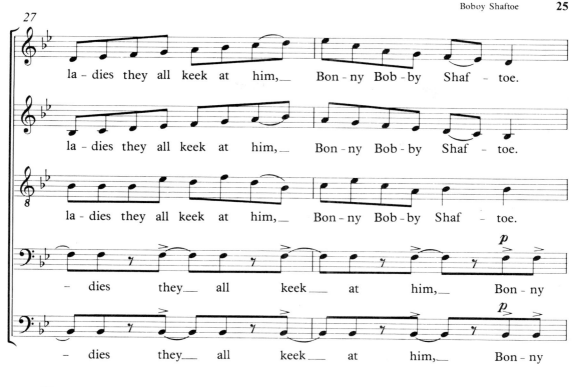

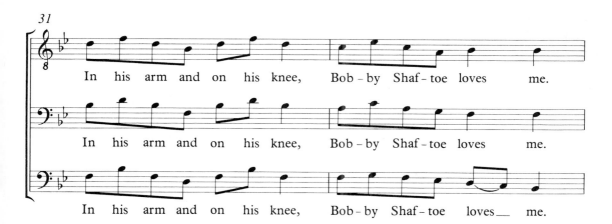

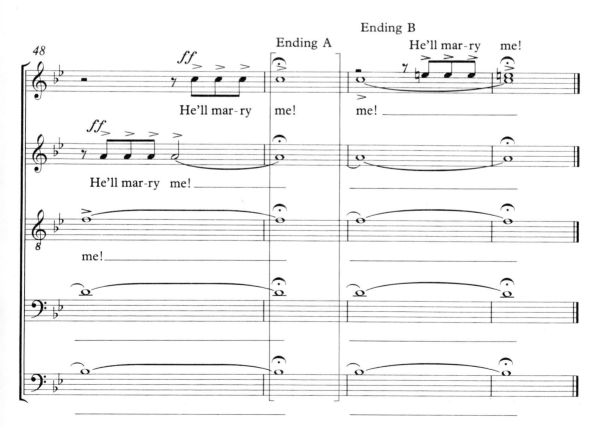

Ending A—for use by single voices.
Ending B—for use by choirs.

5. DASHING AWAY WITH THE SMOOTHING IRON

Traditional song
arranged by
JOHN RUTTER

No. 5 of *Five Traditional Songs* arranged by John Rutter (OUP)

53
Dash - - - - - ing a - way, Dash - -
Dash - - - - - ing a - way Dash - -
Dash-ing a - way with the smooth - ing iron, Dash-ing a - way with the
Dash - - - - - ing a - way, Dash - -
56
mf
- ing a - way, Dash-ing a - way with the iron She
mf
- ing a - way, Dash-ing a - way with the iron She
smooth - ing iron, Dash-ing a - way with the smooth - ing iron She
mf
- ing a - way, Dash-ing a - way with the iron She
59
S.
f
4. 'Twas on a Thurs-day morn - ing And
A.
f
stole my heart a - way. 4. 'Twas on a Thurs-day morn - ing And
T.
f
stole my heart a - way. 4. 'Twas on a Thurs-day morn - ing_ And
Bar.
f
stole my heart a - way. 4. 'Twas_ on a Thurs-day morn - ing_ And
B.
f
stole my heart a - way. 4. 'Twas_ on a Thurs-day morn - ing And

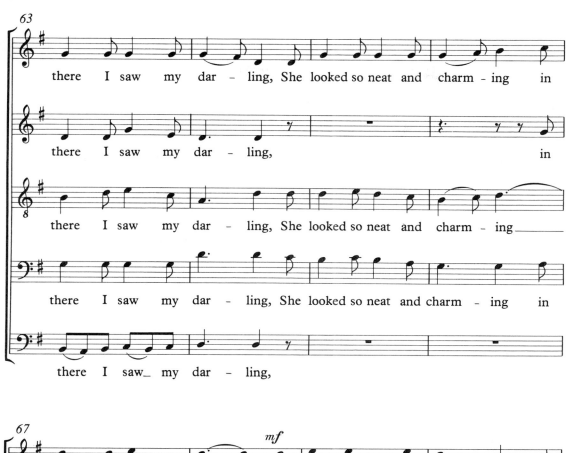

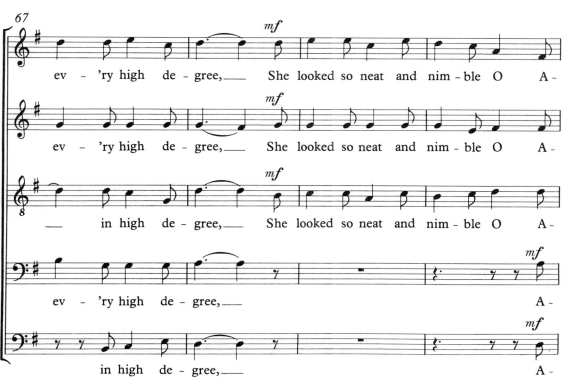

133 **Tempo I**

Dash-ing a-way with the smooth-ing iron,

Dash - ing a - way,

Dash-ing a-way with the smooth-ing iron,

Dash - ing a - way,_____ Dash-ing a-way with the smooth-ing iron,

Dash-ing a - way   with   the smooth - ing iron,

**Presto
(senza rall.)**

137

Dash-ing a-way with the smooth-ing iron   She stole   my heart   a - way.

Dash-ing a-way with the smooth-ing iron   She stole   my heart   a - way.

Dash-ing a-way with the smooth-ing iron   She stole   my heart   a - way.

Dash-ing a-way with the smooth-ing iron   She stole   my heart   a - way.

Dash-ing a-way with the smooth-ing iron   She stole   my heart   a - way.

6. EARLY ONE MORNING

English folk-song
arranged by
DAVID WILLCOCKS

No. 4 of *Five Folk-Songs* arranged by David Willcocks (OUP)

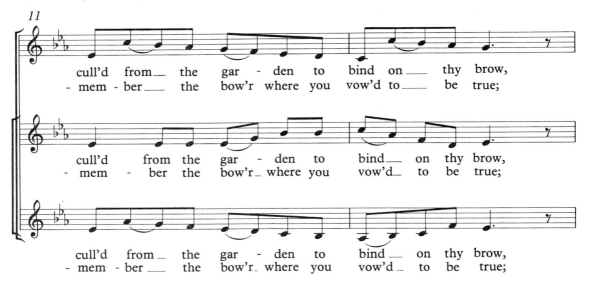

cull'd from __ the gar - den to bind on __ thy brow,
- mem - ber __ the bow'r where you vow'd to __ be true;

cull'd from the gar - den to bind __ on thy brow,
- mem - ber the bow'r __ where you vow'd __ to be true;

cull'd from __ the gar - den to bind __ on thy brow,
- mem - ber __ the bow'r __ where you vow'd __ to be true;

Oh, don't de - ceive me, Oh, ne - ver leave me!

Oh, don't de - ceive __ me, Oh, ne - ver leave __ me!

Oh, don't de - ceive me, Oh, ne - ver leave me!

How __ could you use a poor mai - den so?'

How __ could you use __ a __ poor __ mai - den so?'

How could you use a poor mai - den so?'

VERSE 4 **Poco meno mosso**

to the Henley Choir

7. GREENSLEEVES

English traditional song
arranged by
R. VAUGHAN WILLIAMS

8. LONDONDERRY AIR

('Old Irish tune, wordless and nameless')

Irish melody
arranged by
PERCY GRAINGER

*Sing on *Ah* or any comfortable vowel, and get the tone as rich as possible.

9. MY SWEETHEART'S LIKE VENUS

English translation
by
STEUART WILSON

Welsh folk-song
arranged by
G. HOLST

This needs an easy rhythm, not staccato, otherwise it is too jerky for the sentiment.
There are no indications of tempo or of expression. These will arise out of the singing of the song, and are left to the judgement of the conductor and the singers.   G.H.

VERSE 2

10. O WALY, WALY

Somerset folk-song
arranged by
JOHN RUTTER

No. 2 of *Five Traditional Songs* arranged by John Rutter (OUP)

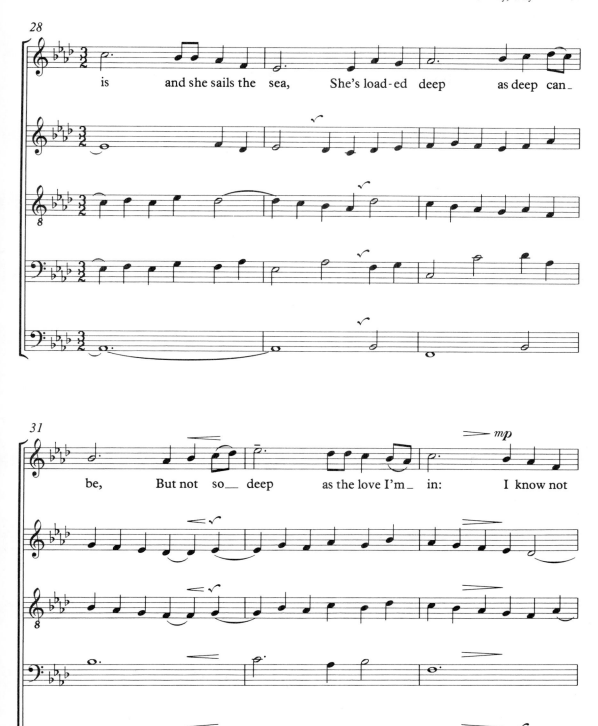

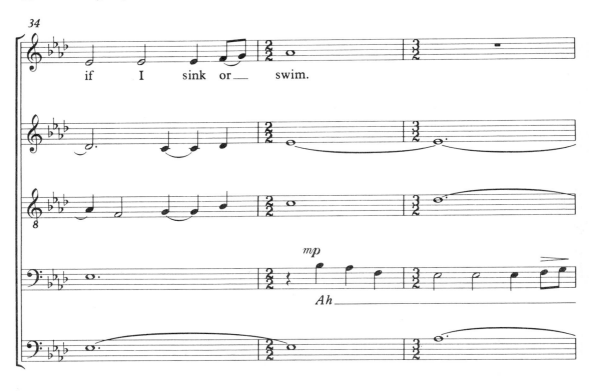

11. SHE'S LIKE THE SWALLOW

Newfoundland folk-song
arranged by
EDWARD T. CHAPMAN

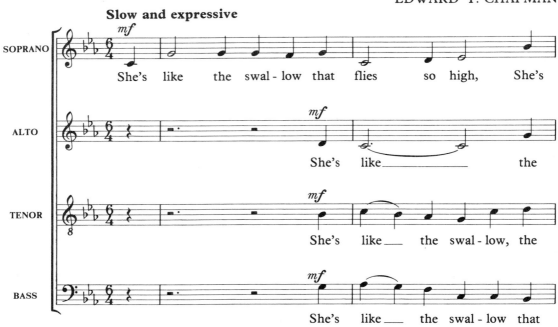

Melody and words from *Folk Songs from Newfoundland*, collected and edited by Maud Karpeles

*If voices are available

12. SOURWOOD MOUNTAIN

Tennessee folk-song
arranged by
JOHN RUTTER

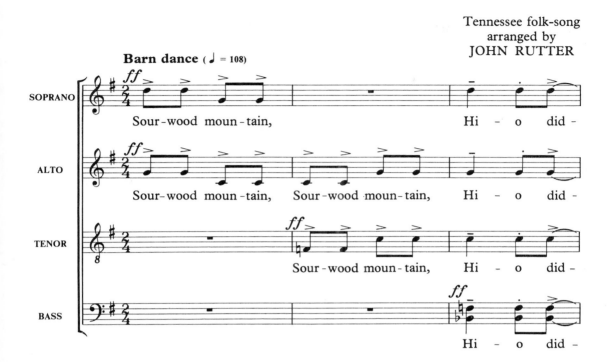

*quasi double-bass pizzicato

This song, together with *Black sheep* (p. 16) may be performed as part of a set of three American folk-songs arranged by John Rutter, with *Down by the riverside* (piano or orchestral accompaniment – X 248) as the final song in the group.

Sourwood Mountain and *Black sheep* are available separately as *Two American folk-songs* – X 247.